THE CIRCLE ⊙F JEWISH LIFE

JOEL LURIE GRISHAVER

TORAH AURA PRODUCTIONS

Torah Aura Productions • 4423 Fruitland Avenue, Los Angeles, CA 90058
(800) BE-Torah • (800) 238-6724 • (323) 585-7312 • fax (323) 585-0327
E-MAIL <misrad@torahaura.com> • Visit the Torah Aura website at www.torahaura.com

ISBN 10   1-891662-90-2

ISBN 13   978-1-891662-90-4

MANUFACTURED IN MALAYSIA

Table of Contents

The Circle of Life

At the beginning of *The Lion King*, Simba is born. All of the animals in the jungle gather and sing "The Circle of Life."

How is life a circle? _____

_____

A Jewish Life

When we go through the Circle of Jewish life we are reliving moments that have happened to other Jews. Put these moments in the order in which they happen in our lives, not by their order in the Bible. (Hint: First we are born.)

_____ Rabbi Akiva began to study Torah at the age of forty.

_____ (According to a midrash) Abraham was thirteen years old when he smashed his father's idols.

_____ Adam and Eve were the first married couple.

_____ Abraham bought a cave so that he could bury his dead wife Sarah.

_____ On the eighth day after he was born, Abraham's son was circumcised.

_____ Moses gave three major sermons to the Jewish people when he was one hundred-and twenty years old.

_____ Abraham and Sarah waited a long time but they finally gave birth to a son, Isaac.

The Tree

It is a Jewish custom to plant a tree on the day when a baby is born. As the child grows, the tree grows. When that child is ready to get married the parents cut branches from the tree and use them to hold up the _huppah_, the wedding canopy.

This custom is a ritual. A ritual is a way of expressing deep ideas or even stories through actions.

1. What does this ritual say to the parents of a newborn baby?
2. What does this ritual say to the parents of a child who is ready to get married?
3. How does this ritual help to show that life is a circle?

© IMAGES.COM/CORBIS

Birth: Entering the Covenant

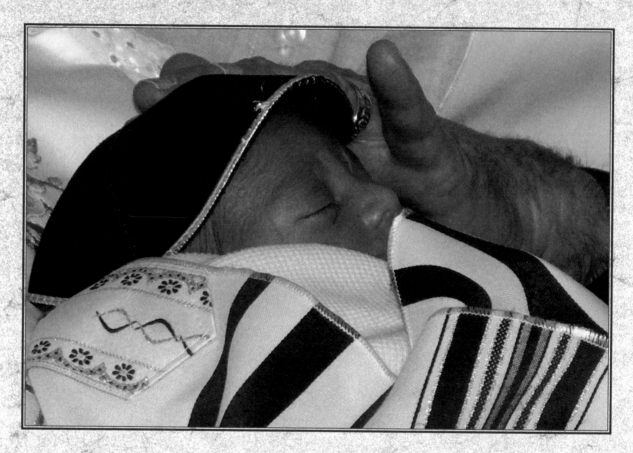

According to the Talmud, God sends an angel to each womb to teach a baby all the wisdom that can be obtained. Just before the baby is born, the angel touches the space between the upper lip and the nose and all that it has taught the baby is forgotten. *(Niddah 30b)*

1. What does this story teach about the purpose of life?
2. What does this story teach about learning?
3. What does this story teach about being a newborn?

Birth Story

Shalom Zakhar

After a Jewish child is born there are lots of celebrations. The first one takes place on the *Erev Shabbat* (Friday Night) right after the baby is born. Traditionally this was only for boys and it was called *Shalom Zakhar*, but today a number of families observe a girls' version of the celebration called **Shalom Nekeivah**. Believe it or not, the big thing about these celebrations is the eating of **chickpeas**.

Brit Milah/Simhat Bat

Eight days after a boy is born there is a ceremony of circumcision called *Brit Milah*. At this ceremony the *k'vater/kvaterin* (one of the godparents) brings the boy into the room and hands him to a parent who hands it to the *sandek* (another godparent). Traditionally, the *sandek* sits in **Elijah's Chair**. The *Brit Milah* ceremony is performed by a *mohel*, a person specially trained to do this minor surgery. Today, in some communities a woman, a *mohellet*, performs the circumcision and leads the service. The community is invited, and a *minyan* (ten people) is needed. After the *Brit Milah*, there is a *Se'udat Mitzvah*, a meal celebrating the performance of this mitzvah.

While the *Brit Milah* is a ceremony for boys, today many families celebrate a parallel ceremony for girls called *Brit*

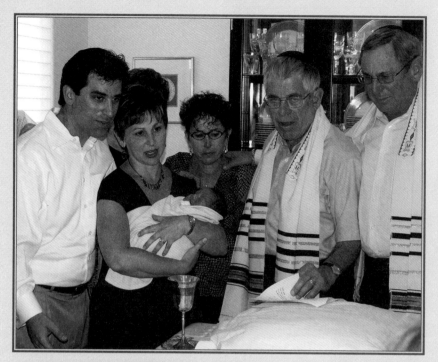

parents of boys have adopted from parents of girls.

Pidyon ha-Ben/ K'dushat Pehter Rehem

Thirty days after a **first** son is born, there is a ceremony called *Pidyon ha-Ben*, which means, "redemption of the firstborn." This is a biblical ceremony in which a father buys back his son from Temple service from a priest (*kohein*). Not all Jews observe this ceremony. And as with other ceremonies that were previously "for boys only," a girl's or non-gender-specific version has been created called *K'dushat Pehter Rehem* (the holiness of the firstborn).

Bat or *Simhat Bat*. Because *Simhat Bat* is a new ceremony, there is no fixed ritual and many families write their own service. There is a *Se'udat Mitzvah* after this *simhah* (happy occasion), too.

Naming

While a boy is ususally given his Hebrew name at a *Brit Milah*, it is a custom to name girls in synagogue on a Shabbat following their birth. Now girls are frequently named at their Simhat Bat, but still it has become a custom for boys and girls to be brought to synagogue to be named (or renamed) in front of the entire congregation on a Shabbat. This is a custom that

Shalom Zakhar: Howdy, Kid

In the Talmud it is written:

Rabbi Isaac quoted Rabbi Ammi, who stated: "As soon as a male comes into the world peace comes into the world." This teaching was translated into a traditional ceremony called שָׁלוֹם זָכָר, *Shalom Zakhar*. This is a "peace comes into the world party" because it is a boy. Or it could be a "welcome son party." שָׁלוֹם *Shalom* can mean "peace" or "hello". *Shalom* is also a name of God.

In her book *How to Run a Jewish Household*, Blu Greenberg suggests that a *Shalom Bat* ceremony should be added to Jewish tradition for newborn girls.

These celebrations are parties held on *Erev Shabbat* (Friday night). The special food that is served at them is chickpeas. These chickpeas tell a story.

The Chickpea Story

Before children are born they learn the whole Torah. Just before birth an angel touches them on the lip, making the line that goes from the middle of the lip to just under the nose. This touch makes them forget everything they have learned. A newborn has to start learning all over again. The chickpea is shaped like a circle and it teaches that life is a circle of learning and forgetting, of happiness and sadness, of living and dying.

Noah to Abraham to You

At the end of the flood, under the rainbow, God told Noah:

*I now make my **brit** with you*
and with your family after you...
never again will all life be destroyed by the waters of a flood...
I give my rainbow in the clouds
*that will be the sign of the **brit**...* (Genesis 9.9-13)

12

After God changed Abram's name to Abraham, God told him:

> I set up my **brit** for Me and for you
> and your future family after you…
> Circumcise every male.
> It will be the sign of the **brit** between me and you.
> When he is eight days old, each boy should be circumcised." *(Genesis 17.10)*

During the *Brit Milah* ceremony it is said:

> Even as this child has been entered into the **brit**
> so may this child be entered into the Torah, the ḥuppah (wedding canopy)
> and a life of good deeds.

A *brit* is a covenant. A covenant is an agreement between two people, a deal. A *brit milah* is a circumcision. It is "a covenant of the flesh".

1. The first **brit** was between God and humanity. It was made with Noah and his family. What did God promise? _Never again will all life be destroyed by waters of a flood._

2. The next **brit** in the Torah was between God and the Jewish people. God made it with Abraham. What did God ask Abraham to promise? _When a boy is eight days old, each boy should be circumcised._

3. What other things connect to the **brit milah** ceremony? _____

_____

13

Making Your Own Brit with God

Every person has a **brit** with God. The Jewish people have a strong **brit** with God. What are some of the promises in your *brit*?

I promise God that:

1. _____
2. _____
3. _____
4. _____

5. _____

I believe that God has promised me that:

1. _____
2. _____
3. _____
4. _____
5. _____

The Brit Milah Ceremony

© MICHAEL FREEMAN/CORBIS

Algerian Jews performing circumcision ceremony, 19th century

A traditional *Brit Milah* looks like this.

I.

The *brit milah* service traditionally takes place on the eighth day after a boy is born. The *kvatterin* and/or the *kvatter* brings the child into the room. These titles come from the German word for godparent. When the child enters the room everyone says:

בָּרוּךְ הַבָּא *Barukh ha-Ba* (Welcome son).

II.

The parent(s) says the prayer below and hands the child to the *mohel*. The *mohel* is a learned Jew who is specially trained to perform the surgery. In Biblical times a father circumcised his own son. Now a father gives this job to someone who is specially trained. This prayer is said:

Parent(s): I am ready to perform the mitzvah of *brit milah* as God made it a mitzvah for us in the Torah, saying: "Throughout your generations every male shall be circumcised when he is eight days old."

15

III.

The parent hands the child to the *mohel*. The *mohel* traditionally placed the child on a pillow on the lap of the *sandek* who is sitting on a chair designated as **Elijah's chair**. The title *sandek* comes from a Greek word for godfather. Elijah was a prophet who did not die, who went directly up to heaven, and who is invited to every Passover seder and every *brit milah*. The *mohel* says an introduction and a blessing. Then the *mohel* performs the surgery. This causes the boy very little pain because of the wine he has been given and because his nerves are not yet fully developed.

> Mohel: This is the chair of Elijah, O Eternal. I hope for your redemption. I wait for your deliverance. I perform your mitzvot. Blessed are you, Eternal our God, Ruler of the Cosmos, the One who makes us holy with mitzvot and made it a mitzvah for us to perform *Brit Milah*.

IV.

The parent(s) then say a blessing:

> Parent(s): Blessed are You, Eternal,
> our God, Ruler of the
> Cosmos, Who sanctified us
> with mitzvot and made it
> a mitzvah for us to enter
> our son into the *brit* of
> Abraham.

Then the *minyan* responds:

> Minyan: Just as he has been entered
> into the *brit*, so may he
> be entered into Torah,
> <u>h</u>uppah (marriage) and a
> life of good deeds.

> Mohel: Blessed are you, Eternal,
> our God, Ruler of the
> Cosmos, Who sanctified us
> with mitzvot and made it
> a mitzvah for us to enter
> our son into the *brit* of
> Abraham.

> Blessed are you, Eternal,
> our God, Ruler of the
> Cosmos, Who made the well loved Isaac holy from birth... and connected
> his descendants with the sign of the *brit*...

> Our God and God of our ancestors, preserve this child for his mother and
> father, and let his name be called in Israel _____.

Everyone joins in the **Se'udat Mitzvah.**

1. Why do you think that this ceremony depends on two kinds of godparents (the *k'vatter* and the *sandek*)? Why don't the parents do it all?
2. Why do you think that this ceremony takes a *minyan*? Why isn't it a private family event?
3. Why is Elijah invited to this ceremony?
4. Why is *Brit Milah* called the Covenant of Abraham?

An Elijah Story

A Moroccan Folk Tale: There was a couple who really wanted a child, but years went by without their wish being fulfilled. So the two of them alone prepared a Passover seder for just two. On Passover eve they sat at their table, reading from the Haggadah when a knock came at the door. The couple opened the door and saw an old man dressed in rags. They invited him in to join their seder, quoting the Haggadah, "Let all who are hungry, come and eat." The three of them prayed, sang, and ate together. They had a wonderful time. The couple said to the man, "We wish that sometime in the future we will be able to spend another seder eve together." The man then asked them, "You two have long wanted a child?" They nodded, yes. Then the man said, "I wish that in the future that your 'seder' (order) will become 'i-seder (chaos)'." Then he left.

Less than a year later, the couple gave birth to a child. Another year later, when Passover came, they prepared a seder for two plus a child on a lap. They began their seder and heard a knock on the door. They opened it to find the same beggar. There was the joy of reunion. The couple was happy that their wish from that previous seder had come true. As they sat at the table their child spilled a cup of wine and began crying. When that was taken care of the child ripped a page from the Haggadah. With that under control the child started crying again. The parents worked hard to keep their child happy and to create good Passover memories. All of a sudden both of them realized that their guest was Elijah and that his wish for chaos had brought them a baby. The four of them had a wonderful seder. Then Elijah left again.

1. What is the lesson of this story?
2. Why is Elijah invited to every *brit milah* ceremony?

Simhat Bat Ceremony

There is no such thing as an official *Brit Bat* or *Simhat Bat* ceremony. Many families write their own. Here are some pieces of one that was written in 1987.

Rabbi: May she who comes be blessed, Avital.

Reverence for life has been given to us as part of our covenant with God, as it is written: "And God said to Israel, 'Choose life, that you and your descendants may live.'" The birth of a daughter brings us joy and hope, and the courage to reaffirm our enduring covenant with life and its Creator.

Mother: (Lights one candle and takes the baby.)

Blessed are You, Our God, Ruler of the Universe, who does good for the undeserving, and who has dealt kindly with us all. May the One who bestows upon you good, continue to bestow upon you good. Let it be so! Joyfully I bring my daughter into the covenant of Israel, a covenant with God, with Torah, and with life. Blessed are You, Eternal our God, Ruler of the Universe, Who sanctified us with mitzvot and commanded us to sanctify life…

Father: (Lights one candle and takes the baby.)

We asked God for life, and a new soul from God was placed within us. Our God and God of our fathers and mothers, Who has not withdrawn goodness from us, bless our daughter… We are privileged to educate her to a love of Israel and of humankind, to Torah, wisdom and the respect of God, to the pursuance of peace and of good deeds…

Parents: As it is written, "Her father and mother will rejoice and your birth will bring happiness." Blessed are You, God, Who makes parents to rejoice in their children.

Grandparents: (light one candle and take baby):

Grandmother: Binding ourselves and future generations to the past is a very important concept in Judaism. Many traditions have been dropped but we would like to retrieve one very lovely one that was begun in Germany, as a special honor and tribute for our first grandchild. This tradition was nearly extinguished by the Holocaust, but we should like to advocate its return as a symbol of our love. This wimple, or *mappah*, or a Torah binder, was originally made from the baby's first swaddling clothes. This, then, would follow the child through its life, as the Torah binder was used in the synagogue on the day of naming at *Pidyon ha-Ben*, at *Bar* or *Bat Mitzvah* and at the <u>h</u>uppah. With this wimple we are binding ourselves to some four hundred years in a chain of tradition. Through the wimple we express our great excitement and thrill as we look forward to the days ahead as we and Avital grow together.

(There are pieces for each of the other three grandparents and a prayer said by all them.)

Everyone: Blessed are You, Eternal our God, Ruler of the Universe, Who has given us life, Who sustains us day by day, and who has brought us to this time.

1. How is this ceremony like the traditional *brit milah* ceremony?
2. In what ways is it different?
3. What is the big theme of this *Sim<u>h</u>at Bat* ceremony?
4. What is the big theme of a traditional *Brit Milah*?

Wimples

Here are some traditional wimples.

At a brit milah (bat) the congregation says, "To Torah, to the Huppah (wedding) and to doing good deeds." Can you see that idea in this art?

Create your own wimple in this space.

My Name is...

Not everyone will be able to answer all these questions, but your parents and grandparents can be great resources.

1. My grandparents' names are/were:

    _____

    _____

    _____

    _____

    _____

2. My parents' names are:

    _____

    _____

3. My Jewish name is:_____

    It means: _____

    I am named after: _____

4. A Jewish name identifies not only you but your parents. A Jewish name is:
    _____*Yitzhak*_____ son/daughter of _____*Avraham*_____ and _____*Sarah*_____ .
    A person can always get a Jewish name. It is never too late. If you don't know
    your Jewish name, your teacher, your educator or your rabbi will be happy to
    help you figure yours out.
    My Jewish name is:
    _____ ben/bat _____ v'_____ .

    What my Jewish name means to me: _____

    _____

Family

Here is a midrash about family. It starts with the story of Adam and Eve. When God is about to create Eve, God says: "*It is not good for a person to live alone*" (Gen. 2.18). The midrash then explains what it means to live alone.

It is:

Without help: *I will make for Adam a helpmate who fits with him* (Gen. 2.18).

Without joy: *And you will rejoice, you and your household* (Deut. 14.26).

Without a blessing: *I will cause a blessing to rest on your house* (Ezek. 44.30).

Without atonement: *People should make atonement alone and also for their house.* (Lev. 16.11)

R. Simon said in the name of R. Joshua b. Levi: **Without peace**, *too, for it is said: "And peace will be to your house."* (I Sam. 25.6)

R. Joshua of Siknin said in the name of R. Levi: **Without life,** *too, for it is said, "Enjoy life with the partner whom thou lovest."* (Eccl. 9.9)

R. Hiyya ben Gomdi said: **One is also incomplete**, *for it is written, "And God blessed them, and called them together human."* (Gen. 5.2)

(Genesis Rabbah 17.2)

1. Why is it not good for a person to be alone?
2. This passage lists lots of things that happen in families. What do you think are the three most important?
3. What word does this midrash frequently use for family? What does this word teach?

Mishpahah/Bayit

The modern Hebrew word for family is מִשְׁפָּחָה *mishpahah*. It is a Hebrew word whose root שפח probably started out as the word for boy servant but then came to mean a group of children and then a group with children. The first time it is used in the Bible is in the story of Noah's ark. We are told that each animal left the ark with its *mishpahah*.

The most frequent word for family used in the Bible is the word בַּיִת, *bayit*, household. In the *bayit* you found not only people who are related, but also servants, fellow travelers, and others who were part of this group. A *bayit* was a group of people who made their way through life together.

Think of your family as a group of people who share walls. Then add to it all the other houses that have a connection to yours. Not all families have two parents. Not all families have children. Not everyone in a family need be related. Sometimes families split into two households. Sometimes two households join together. All families have connections and these connections are usually based on people who once lived together. That is how grandparents, cousins, uncles, and aunts are part of our family.

My Family Map

Draw a map of your family. Start with your house. Write in it the names of the people who live there. Pets count, too. Then add in all the other houses with which you are connected.

Family Obligations

Judaism is big on obligations. We believe that the *mitzvot* teach us the way that God wants us to treat each other. In the Talmud there is a discussion of obligations within a family. Here are a few pieces of that discussion.

A FATHER is OBLIGATED
[1] to circumcise his son,
[2] to redeem him [if he is a firstborn,]
[3] to teach him Torah,
[4] to take a wife for him and
[5] to teach him a craft. Some say the father is even obligated
[6] to teach him to swim (Talmud, Kiddushim).

Write your own version of this text:

A MOTHER is OBLIGATED [1] to _____ her daughter,

[2] to _____and

[3] to _____ .

In the Bible we have two similar commandments:

Exodus 20.12: Honor *your father and your mother…*

Leviticus 19.3: Everyone shall revere *his mother and her father…*

In the Talmud the Rabbis explain the difference between **honor** and **reverence** of an aging parent by an adult child:

What is proper reverence *for one's parents and what is proper* honor?

Reverence means that one may not stand in a parent's place and one may not sit in a parent's place. One may not contradict a parent's words, and one may not offer an opinion in a debate to which a parent is a party.

Honor means that one must give a parent food and drink; dress a parent and cover the parent; bring the parent in and take the parent out (Talmud, Kiddushim).

Write your own version of this text

A child should revere *grandparents by [1]* _____

[2] _____ *and [3]* _____.

A child should honor *grandparents by [1]* _____

[2] _____ *and [3]* _____.

The Talmud also talks about relationships between husband and wife:

"Be very careful if you make a woman cry, because God counts her tears (Bava Metzia 59a). The woman came out of a man's rib: Not from his feet to be walked on. Not from his head to be superior, but from the side to be equal. Under the arm to be protected, and next to the heart to be loved" (Philo).

Write your own text about how spouses should treat each other.

_____

_____

_____

_____

_____

_____

_____

The Peace Pudding

A <u>H</u>asidic Story: A husband and wife were fighting. They were in the middle of a big argument. They went to see the Maggid of Koznitz to have him work out a solution. The husband said: "I work hard all week. On Shabbat I want my dessert first, but my wife serves it last after the fish, the soup, the chicken and everything else. After I eat all that I have no room for the dessert, and I want my pudding."

His wife said to the Maggid, "It is wrong to serve desert first. Pudding comes at the end."

Then the Maggid gave his answer "*Sh'lom bayit*, family peace is the most important thing. From now on," he said to the wife, "I want you to make two desserts. You will serve one before the meal and the other you will serve after it." The two of them happily took his advice. From then on the Maggid's wife also made two desserts each and every Shabbat.

1. What is the lesson of this story?
2. What is *Sh'lom bayit* and why is it so important?

28

Jewish Divorce

The Jewish tradition knows that not every marriage will work. Even though couples try hard to love each other, sometimes they have problems that make it impossible to stay husband and wife. Judaism knew that some marriages needed a way to "un-marry." The Jewish version of divorce is called a *get*. A *get* is a religious way of becoming divorced.

A *get* is a traditional form of divorce. It is required by Orthodox Jews. Some Reform Jews do not believe a *get* is necessary. They say that a civil (government) divorce is good enough. They do not demand that divorce also be a religious process. Conservative Jews deal with divorce in two ways. First, they have their own *Bet Din* (a court of three rabbis) to issue a *get*. Second, they have a part of their *ketubah* (marriage contract) called the **Lieberman Clause,** after the scholar who wrote it, that says that the husband promises to give a *get*. **Reconstructionist** Jews have their own *get* that is egalitarian (equal for men and woman) and filled out after the civil divorce.

1. Why does a society that has a form of marriage need a form of divorce?
2. Should divorce be a secular (government) or religious process?

Be a Family Counselor

Here is a situation from the Torah. Be a good family counselor and advise this family what to do.

Abraham was the patriarch of the family. He had two women in his life. The first was Sarah; she was his wife. The second was Hagar. She started out as a servant to Sarah. When Sarah couldn't have children, she gave Hagar to her husband as a "secondary wife" so that he could have a child. When Hagar was pregnant she made fun of Sarah and Sarah kicked her out of the camp. But after a short while Hagar came back. She gave birth to a son named Ishmael. Thirteen years later Sarah finally gave birth, as an old woman, to a son named Isaac. Both boys continued to grow. Ishmael began to play dangerous games with Isaac. Hagar continued to mock Sarah and challenge her status as the number one wife. Sarah asked Abraham again to kick Hagar and her son out of camp.

You Be the Counselor: What should be done?

Portrait of a Divorce

Here is what a traditional *get* ceremony looks like. Surprisingly, there are no prayers.

1. Husband and wife state before the *Bet Din* (court of three rabbis) that they understand what is going to happen and that they are acting freely without being forced.

2. The husband appoints the **sofer** (scribe) to write the twelve-line *get* document. The *get* makes no reference to responsibility or fault. The finished document is signed by witnesses.

3. The signed document is presented to the wife by the husband. Once she accepts it, the divorce takes effect immediately.

4. The *get* document itself remains in the files of the officiating rabbi. It is cut so that it can never be used again.

1. What makes a **get** a religious ceremony?
2. Why are no prayers or blessings said at this ceremony?
3. Is this ceremony fair to women?

Adoption

In the Bible Abraham "adopted" his nephew Lot. There was no ceremony. There was no legal process. Abraham just had Lot join his camp, which was a big extended family.

Jewish life went on that way for a long time. If parents died, a child went to a relative. There was no formal adoption. The child just became part of the new family (but his or her birth parents were still his or her parents). If there were no relatives to be found, the orphan child went to live with a member of the community.

Starting in the 1800s orphanages became wide-spread. Suddenly, as cities grew and small communities broke down, many children without parents were begging on the streets. Along with orphanages adoption became common.

Today, many children who are without families find homes with families who welcome them as new members. Often, couples who are unable to have children grow their families through adoption. While once there was no Jewish ceremony for adoption; today most rabbis will perform a ritual to help parents welcome adopted children into their families.

Conversion

We call people who have become Jewish "Jews by choice". Today, Jews by choice are important members of the Jewish community. Many of them have leadership roles and are actively involved in shaping the Jewish future. If you want to understand conversion to Judaism you need to read the book of Ruth in the Bible.

Narrator: [1.11]And Naomi said,

Naomi: Turn back my daughters. Why will you go with me? Are there yet any more sons in my womb, that they may be your husbands?

Narrator: [14]And they lifted up their voice, and wept again; and Orpah kissed her mother-in-law; but Ruth held fast to her.

[15]And Naomi said,

Naomi: Behold, your sister-in-law has gone back to her people, and to her gods; go back you after your sister-in-law.

Narrator: [16]And Ruth said,

Ruth: Do not ask me to leave you, or to not follow after you; for wherever you go, I will go; and where you lodge, I will lodge; your people shall be my people, and your God my God. [17]Where you die, will I die, and there will I be buried; may the Eternal do so for me....

1. These few verses, especially Ruth's speech, are the blueprint for Jewish conversion. What does it mean to become a Jew?
2. Can you become a Jew by just accepting the "Jewish God"?
3. Based on this text is it easy or hard to become a Jew?

Becoming a Jew by Choice

The process of becoming a Jew by choice differs from place to place, rabbi to rabbi, kind of synagogue to kind of synagogue.

1. Traditionally, a person who wants to become a Jew is turned down three times before he or she is accepted into the process of conversion. Today some branches of Judaism believe in making it easy to begin the conversion process.

2. Becoming a Jew involves a lot of study. Sometimes this is a combination of an Introduction to Judaism course and private study with a rabbi. Sometimes it is just private study.

3. Often the potential Jew goes before a *Bet Din*. Traditionally, this is a court made up of three rabbis. Some Reform and some Reconstructist congregations have a *Bet Din* made up of active congregants.

4. A man who converts to Judaism undergoes *brit milah*. This is not always the case in Reform or Reconstructionist Judaism.

5. Next comes immersion in a *mikvah*. A *mikvah* is a ritual bath. Being totally covered by water and then bursting out is like being reborn.

6. Many synagogues have a public completion of conversion at a ceremony that is performed before the congregation on Shabbat.

Torah Events

The letters of the Torah are sparks and the words are a flame. At every syllable the reader's eye might start a fire. (Edmond Jabes)

Explain this statement in your own words.

_____

_____

_____

_____

Consecration, Bar/Bat Mitzvah, Confirmation and Adult Education

Torah study is something that one can start but can never finish.

In the days of the *shtetl* (Jewish villages in Europe) it was a tradition that fathers would carry their children to the first day of school. A slate with a Hebrew letter written in honey was placed before the child who began Jewish learning by licking the letter. It was a sweet beginning.

Consecration

Today in some synagogues there is a ceremony called **Consecration** that celebrates the beginning of Jewish schooling. First-year students receive a little Torah and a blessing while standing before the open ark. In other synagogues there is a ceremony when students begin studying Hebrew. They are given their own **siddurim**.

© GRAHAM AND GRAHAM

Bar/Bat Mitzvah

When boys turn thirteen and girls turn either twelve-years-six-months or thirteen years old they become a *bar* (boy) or *bat* (girl) *mitzvah*. Soon after that, they are called to the Torah for the first time and publicly celebrate their entering into responsibility for observing the *mitzvot* found in the Torah.

Confirmation

Jewish education does not stop with becoming *bat* or *bar mitzvah*. Some students continue studying in their synagogue and in ninth, tenth, or eleventh grade reach a ceremony called **Confirmation**. Confirmation remembers the time when the Jewish people stood at Mt. Sinai and accepted the Torah. In other synagogues students go on to Hebrew high school. When they finish Hebrew high school they have a **graduation**.

Other Experiences

Jewish summer camps, **Jewish youth groups,** and trips to **Israel** are also part of a Jewish education. Jewish education does not end with high school. In college there is **Hillel**, a Jewish organization, and there are courses in **Jewish Studies**. Jewish learning and Jewish activities can be part of the college experience. But college is not the end of Jewish learning, either.

Adult Learning

There are many opportunities for adult Jewish learning. Many synagogues, Jewish community centers, and other places offer Jewish courses. Some adults become an **adult *bar*** or ***bat mitzvah*** if they never became one as a teenager. And some adults celebrate a **second bar** or **bat mitzvah** at age eighty-three, seventy years after their first one. Jewish learning never stops.

The Torah of Torah Study

Pick a partner and read these three texts. Read them to each other. Explain them to each other. Pick the one you like the best.

[1] Torah Brings You Closer to God

If you work hard in the study of Torah you will be able to understand the hints and meanings contained in all the different things in the world and use them as a means of coming closer to God. Even if you find yourself in a place of darkness where you might think it hard to draw close to God, true wisdom will radiate to you and you will be able to draw close to God even from there [Rabbi Nahman of Bretzlav, Likutei Maharan 1.4].

[2] Torah Helps to Create You

The entire Torah was given to the Jewish people as a whole. However, each person has his or her own particular teaching, a specific goal for his or her life. This is hidden within the soul. When that particular teaching is brought out into the world, that person has reached the truth of his or her being [Sefat Emet, Rabbi Yehudah Aryeh Leib Alter].

[3] Torah Builds Friendships

A hevruta is a person's Torah study partner. It is also one's friend. A hevruta is someone you eat and drink with. A hevruta is someone you study Torah (God's word) with and someone you study Mishnah (ethics and laws) with. A hevruta is someone who sleeps over—or at whose house you can spend the night. Hevrutot (friends) teach each other secrets, the secrets of the Torah— and secrets of the real world, too [Avot d'Rabbi Natan].

Consecration

There were no schools in the days of the Bible. Originally parents taught their own children. In the year 64, a high priest named Joshua ben Gamla realized that not enough children were getting a Torah education. He made it a law that every community had to open a school for its children.

Over one hundred years ago rabbis figured out that it would be good to begin Jewish schooling with a ceremony. They invented **Consecration**. Near the beginning of the year the kindergarten class is invited up on the *bimah*. They are given a blessing by the Rabbi and small Torah scrolls they can keep as a way of remembering.

If you could whisper one piece of advice about going to a Jewish school to a student in the Consecration Class, what would it be? _____

_____

The Bar/Bat Mitzvah Blessing

© TED SPIEGEL/CORBIS

Bar and *bat mitzvah* happen by the calendar. When a boy turns thirteen years and a day old, he is a *bar mitzvah*. When a girl reaches either twelve years, six months, and a day, or thirteen years and a day old, she is a *bat mitzvah*. (More traditional Jews go by the earlier date). There is also a traditional blessing and a more modern blessing for parents of a *bar* or *bat mitzvah*.

Traditional Blessing

בָּרוּךְ שֶׁפְּטָנִי מֵעָנְשׁוֹ שֶׁלָזֶה.

Blessed is the One Who has liberated me (from the responsibility for) the wrong things that this child does.

Modern Blessing

בָּרוּךְ אַתָּה יי אֱלֹהֵינוּ מֶלֶךְ הָעוֹלָם שֶׁהֶחֱיָנוּ וְקִיְּמָנוּ וְהִגִּיעָנוּ לַזְּמַן הַזֶּה.

Blessed are You, Eternal our God, the One Who gives us life, sustains us, and brings us to this (special) moment.

1. How does the traditional blessing look at becoming *bar/bar mitzvah*?
2. How does the modern blessing look at becoming *bar/bar mitzvah*?
3. Which one do you prefer? Why?

Why Does Bar/Bat Mitzvah Happen at Thirteen?

A *bar/bat mitzvah* should be able to control the *yetzer ha-ra*, the impulse to do evil, and that is what makes a child ready to be responsible for the *mitzvot*.

© FRANCIS G. MAYER/CORBIS

The yetzer ha-ra (impulse to do evil): What is that? It is said: The yetzer ha-ra is thirteen years older than the yetzer ha-tov (impulse to do good). People are born being selfish, not thinking about others, getting angry, and doing other things that can hurt other people. As people grow and learn, things like sharing, waiting one's turn, helping others, and other things learned through experience and from friends, teachers and parents. By the time a child is thirteen she or he should be ready to set limits on the yetzer ha-ra and know how to reach out to do good (Avot de Rabbi Natan 16:2).

1. How would you explain the *yetzer ha-ra*?
2. Why does it take longer to develop the *yetzer ha-tov*?
3. Why is thirteen the right time to make a child responsible for the *mitzvot*?
4. Which of the two parental *bar mitzvah* blessings (previous page) uses this understanding?

The Tallit

A *tallit* is a garment with four corners with a specially knotted fringe in each corner. Traditionally a boy would begin wearing a *tallit katan* (a small tallit) when that child was toilet trained. A *tallit katan* is a square of fabric with a hole in the center that is worn over an undershirt and usually under a regular shirt. A *tallit gadol* (a big *tallit*) was sometimes first worn at a bar mitzvah sometimes first worn for a marriage ceremony. Originally wearing a *tallit* was just a *mitzvah* for men. Today, outside of Orthodox Judaism, many women wear *tallitot*.

Here are four designer *tallitot*.

Csilla Balogh

Reeva Shaffer

Reeva's 'writing with Ruach

Design your own Tallit

"What Is The Most Important Verse in the Torah?"

What is the most important verse in the Torah?

> *Rabbi Akiva said: "'You shall love your neighbor as yourself.' This is a great principle of the Torah."*

> *Ben Azzai disagreed: "The verse 'This is the book of the descendants of Adam…the human whom God made in God's likeness'* (Genesis 5:1). *This is a principle even greater"* (Jerusalem Talmud, Nedarim 9:4, 41c).

Bar/Bat Mitzvah students deliver a *d'var Torah* (a Torah talk). Pick one of these two verses and write a d'var Torah that explains it.

A Bar/Bat Mitzvah Looks Like This

A *bar* or *bat mitzvah* is a person, not an event. Traditionally, when a boy turned thirteen years old and a day, or when a girl reached twelve years and six months and a day, they were legally responsible for the *mitzvot*. This made them a *bar* or a *bat mitzvah*. Originally, this ceremony was only for boys. They started out by calling the boy up to the Torah for a single *aliyah* to show the whole community that he was old enough. Most people say that the first *bat mitzvah* ceremony was held for Judith Kaplan, daughter of Reconstructionism's founder Rabbi Mordecai Kaplan, in 1922. However, there is evidence of earlier synagogue celebrations for girls in Italy, France, and Poland. But *bat mitzvah* ceremonies became regular events only in the twentieth century.

More or less a *bar* or *bat mitzvah* ceremony looks like this:

1. The *bat/bar mitzvah* leads all or some of the service.

2. The parents present the son or daughter with a *tallit*.

3. The family participates in the Torah service. Sometimes the Torah is passed through generations of the family down to the *bar/bat mitzvah*.

4. The *bar/bat mitzvah* reads Torah and has an **aliyah** (a Torah honor) —usually **maftir** (the last honor) and also reads **haftarah** (a matching selection from the Prophets).

5. The *bar/bat mitzvah* student presents a **d'var Torah**, a talk on the Torah portion.

6. Afterward the community celebrates the mitzvah with a **s'udat mitzvah**.

Acting like An Adult

At your *bar* or *bat mitzvah* ceremony you do not become an adult, but you do become responsible for beginning to act like an adult. Here is a collection of *middot*. *Middot* are the values that the Torah wants us to use to guide our life. Pick the three that you think are most important.

_____ Repentence (תְּשׁוּבָה *T'shuvah*)

_____ Forgiveness (סְלִיחָה *S'liḥah*)

_____ Loving Your Neighbor (וְאָהַבְתָּ לְרֵעֲךָ כָּמוֹךָ *V'ahavta l'Reyakha Kamokhah*)

_____ Controlling Anger (אֶרֶךְ אַפַּיִם *Erekh Apayim*)

_____ Doing the Right Thing (דֶּרֶךְ אֶרֶץ *Derekh Eretz*)

_____ Groundless Hate (שִׂנְאַת-חִנָּם *Sinat Ḥinam*)

_____ Being a Friend (חַבְרוּתָא *Ḥevruta*)

_____ Pursuing Peace (רוֹדֵף שָׁלוֹם *Rodef Shalom*)

_____ Preventing Shame (בּוּשָׁה *Bushah*)

_____ Taking Care of Your Body (שְׁמִירַת הַגּוּף *Sh'mirat ha-Guf*)

_____ Guarding One's Tongue (שְׁמִירַת הַלָּשׁוֹן *Sh'mirat ha-Lashon*)

Standing at Sinai

There is a midrashic idea that all Jews from all of time escaped from Egypt and all Jews from all of time stood at Mt. Sinai and accepted the Torah.

The students of the Holy Maggid of Mezerich described his teaching this way. "He got each of us to tell our own story of what it was like to go out of Egypt and our own story of what it was like to stand at Mount Sinai" (Martin Buber, Tales of the Ḥasidim).

1. Why is it important for Jews to "remember" that they were personally taken out of Egypt and stood at Mount Sinai?
2. Who were you standing next to at Sinai?
3. What did God's voice sound like?
4. What one thing do you remember most?

Confirmation and Shavuot

The Jewish people gathered at the foot of Mount Sinai and God spoke the Ten Commandments from the top of the mountain. Before God gave a single commandment, the Jewish people said, נַעֲשֶׂה וְנִשְׁמַע "*Na'aseh V'Nishma*" (We will do and we will listen). Jewish Bible commentators have always made a big deal out of their saying "We will do" before they said "We will listen". This is like signing a contract before you read it or know what is in it. That is how much the Jews trusted God. The Jewish holiday of Shavuot takes place on the date on which the Torah was given.

Confirmation takes place on or near Shavuot. It celebrates the giving and the accepting of the Torah. At Confirmation, just as at Mount Sinai, the Confirmation class says "*Na'aseh v'Nishma*."

On Shavuot we read the *Book of Ruth*. Ruth was a Moabite woman who chose to become a Jew. After her husband died and her mother-in-law decided to return to Israel, Ruth told her "Do not ask me to leave you, or to not follow after you; for wherever you go, I will go; and where you lodge, I will lodge; your people shall be my people, and your God my God; where you die, will I die, and there will I be buried; may the Eternal do so for me…" On Shavuot the confirmands act like Ruth and pledge a commitment to Judaism.

48

Check Off the Top Three Jewish Things You Will Pledge

_____ I believe in One God.

_____ I will support Israel.

_____ I will live an ethical life.

_____ I will study Torah.

_____ I will celebrate Shabbat and other Jewish
　　　　 holidays.

_____ I will have a Jewish home.

_____ I will help make the world better.

_____ I will say the _Shema_ at bedtime.

_____ I will remember that I was created
　　　　 in God's image.

_____ I will feel connected to all Jews.

Gabriel's Ark

Sandra R. Curtis, Ph.D.

When Gabriel was born a rainbow was in the sky. The rainbow was his sign of welcome. When he was born he was small and weak. "He won't grow or learn like other children," his doctor told his parents that day almost thirteen years ago.

"Guess who's hiding in the ark?" Rachel and Leah, his sisters, asked. Gabriel loved playing with his toy ark. He liked guessing what animals his sisters put inside. His sisters often played this hiding game with Gabe. They liked planning the surprise and Gabe looked forward to seeing which of his favorite animals would be hiding in the ark.

Gabriel's mother lit the Sabbath candles that Friday evening and the family sat down to dinner. "Gabe will be thirteen soon," she said. "Papa and I are planning a special *bar mitzvah* service with Rabbi Cohen." Gabriel started to cry. "No rabbi! No service!"

"Gabe," his mother said gently, "remember we talked about this? It's a tradition for Jewish children when they turn thirteen. And you like Rabbi Cohen. He tells stories, like your favorite, Noah's ark. He wants you to bring your animals."

Gabe became quiet. "My ark?" "That, too," his mother smiled.

On Sunday Gabriel's family visited the synagogue.

50

"Hi, Gabe." The rabbi smiled. "What's in your bag?"

"My ark," Gabriel answered shyly.

"Can I see your ark?" asked the rabbi.

As Gabe took out his toy and set up the animals, a funny smile crossed his face. "Hide,"

he said. And he made the rabbi guess what animal was inside.

"Now let's see what's hiding in my ark," said Rabbi Cohen. He peeked inside the doors of the *Aron Kodesh*. He opened the ark to reveal two Torah scrolls. "Each of these scrolls contains the stories and laws of the Jewish people," he explained. "Your Noah story is in here. Come see. That's Hebrew. You hold the pointer, and I'll read. 'It rained for forty days and forty nights. Water covered the entire earth. When the rain finally stopped and the water went down, God set a rainbow in the sky as a promise never to destroy life on earth again.'"

"We need a really big rainbow over the ark," said Rachel, "so we remember that promise. I can draw it."

"If you do, I'll put it up," the rabbi promised. Then he knelt beside Gabe and sang a familiar prayer, the *Shema*. "Your sisters are going to say this prayer with you at your *Bar Mitzvah*."

As Gabe marched his animals back into the ark, the rabbi spoke softly. "When we recite the *Shema*, we're declaring that we are one people, the people Israel, and we have one God. You are part of that people, Gabe, like everyone in your family."

"For My house shall be called a house of prayer for all peoples" was written over the door to the synagogue. "Isaiah, the prophet, said that," explained Rabbi Cohen. "We want everyone to feel welcome here. Each of us is special in his own way, because we are all created in God's image. We should feel as safe in here as the animals did in the ark."

The following Saturday bustled with excitement. Everyone dressed early in their Sabbath best. . . everyone except Gabriel.

"Better pack your animals, Gabe," Papa coaxed. "They want to see Rabbi Cohen, because it's *your* special day and he's going to tell *their* special story." Once the animals were safely in their bag, Gabriel let his father help him dress. A rainbow of balloons greeted the family when they arrived at the synagogue. It arched over the entrance at the top of the new ramp.

"It's our sign of welcome," said Mother.

The service began. Gabe played with his animals. When he got restless, his father took him outside. "It's almost time to say your prayer," Papa said. "Remember Rabbi Cohen's promise. We're all here to help." Gabe and his sisters opened the doors of the *Aron Kodesh.* The rabbi lifted the Torah, and the girls began to sing. Gabriel, however, remained silent. "Hear, O Israel..." his sisters continued alone.

"Let's read Noah's story," smiled Rabbi Cohen, offering Gabriel his hand.

"Wait," Gabe whispered. He picked up his toy ark and slowly looked at the Torah before him.

"Hear Israel. One God. Rainbow promise."

The congregation rose and watched the family pass the Torah from generation to generation beneath Rachel's rainbow.

1. What is the big lesson of this story?
2. What does this story teach about Torah study?
3. How does your synagogue express Isaiah's teaching: "For My house shall be called a house of prayer for all peoples"?

Whole-Life Learning

Match the picture at the bottom with its description. Write the number of the picture you would put in each box.

3 Schools are not the only places to learn about Judaism. Many Jewish children go to Jewish camps. These are places where they can play sports and learn Israeli dances; where they can go swimming and have Jewish programs; and where they can sleep out under the stars and sing Jewish songs. Jewish camps are great places to have fun and do Jewish learning.

☐ A Jewish youth group is a collection of Jewish kids who do things together. Sometimes they can go bowling or go away for a weekend. Sometimes they collect food for a food bank or celebrate a Jewish holiday. The best part about a youth group is that it gives you a chance to be part of a Jewish community.

☐ There is nowhere like Israel. Israel is a Jewish state. It is a place where people speak Hebrew. But, most of all, it is a place to see, touch, walk, eat, swim, climb, and enjoy the story of the Jewish people. In Israel you can see the places where the Bible took place and you can meet Jewish people from all over the world. In Israel all of the Jewish tradition is alive. You can visit Israel in high school or college (or even as an adult).

In college there is Hillel. Hillel is a Jewish organization that holds parties and classes, a place to eat kosher food, and enjoy all kinds of programs. Participating in Hillel is one way you can connect with your Judaism in college. Taking Jewish courses at your university is another way. Another thing you can do during college is have a Jewish job. You can teach, tutor, work as a Jewish youth group advisor, or be a counselor at a Jewish camp. Jewish learning does not have to stop when you leave home.

Grownups can continue their Jewish learning, too. There are loads of Jewish organizations to join, many places to take Jewish classes, and a world of Jewish books and magazines to read. There are adult Jewish camps, trips to Israel, and more kinds of Jewish learning experiences from Torah study and mountain climbing to a Jewish music cruise.

And of course, families can study Torah together, too. They can do it at home on their own. They can do it at family programs and family schools. Families can go to camp and to Israel together. Jewish learning is for everyone.

Marriage

A Roman woman asked Rabbi Yosi, "You say that your God created the universe. What has your God been doing since then?"

"God has been arranging marriages," Rabbi Yosi replied.

"Is that all? Anyone can do that!" To prove her point, the woman returned home and lined up all her male and female servants, pairing them up and marrying them off. The following morning two servants knocked on her door, beaten and bruised, and complained, "I do not want the spouse you assigned me."

The woman came back to Rabbi Yosi and said, "Matchmaking is a very difficult thing to do right. It probably takes the Creator of the universe."

1. What does this story teach about God?
2. What does this story teach about marriage?

Getting Married

At a Jewish wedding a couple exchanges rings and says:

הֲרֵי אַתְּ/אַתָּה מְקֻדֶּשֶׁת/מְקֻדָּשׁ לִי בְּטַבַּעַת זוֹ כְּדַת מֹשֶׁה וְיִשְׂרָאֵל.

Behold, with this ring you are set apart for just me

According to the Law of Moses and Israel.

A wedding ceremony connects two people together. The first marriage was between Adam and Eve.

Finding Each Other

Today we believe in falling in love first, then getting married. Once Jews believed in getting married and then falling in love. Jews used to use a *shadkhan*, a matchmaker, to arrange marriages. Some Jews still do. There are lots of other ways of meeting the person you will marry. Some people meet by accident or in school. Other people go on-line and find a person to love on **JDate** or other places on the Internet. Finding each other may be the hardest part of getting married.

The Jewish Wedding

Jewish weddings are a little bit complicated. There are three parts to a traditional Jewish wedding: *Shiddukhin*, the engagement, *erusin*, the betrothal; and *nissuim*, the "wedding" part. Once these three ceremonies took place on three different dates. Today, *shiddukhin* (from the same root as *shadkhan*, matchmaker) happens only in the Orthodox world. The other two ceremonies have been compressed into one series of events that happen on the same day.

Shiddukhin

In the days when parents used a *shadkhan* to find the right match for their son or daughter, there was a ceremony in which the "deal" for the wedding was agreed upon. This was often the

day that the husband-and wife-to-be met for first time. The parents would then sign the *tennaim*, the conditions. The *tennaim* represent a contract to have the wedding. Next the *ḥatan* (groom) and *kallah* (bride) would exchange gifts. He would give her a couple of items (nothing specific being called for). She would give him a *tallit* and a *kittel*. A *kittel* is a special white garment worn at a wedding, worn on every Yom Kippur, worn at every Passover seder, and worn as the garment the man will be buried in. The *kittel* traces a mini-life cycle.

Before the Wedding

Before the wedding it is traditional for the *kallah* to go the *mikvah*. The *mikvah* is a ritual bath. Some Jewish women go to the *mikvah* every month. Some Jewish men use a *mikvah* as a place of spiritual preparation. A *kallah* uses the *mikvah* as a way of getting ready for the wedding. On the Shabbat before the wedding is an *aufruf*. This is when a couple is called up to the Torah for an *aliyah* (honor) in synagogue. After the *aliyah* the congregation throws candy at them. The candy is a wish for a sweet life. It is the Jewish version of rice at a wedding.

Once, the *aufruf* was just an *aliyah* for men. Today, except in Orthodox synagogues, it is usually for *hatan* and *kallah*.

Day of the Wedding

The day of the wedding is like a mini-Yom Kippur for the *hatan* and *kallah*. They fast and prepare themselves for a day on which they will start their lives over in a new way. It was a tradition for the *hatan* and the *kallah* not to see each other for the week before the wedding. On the day of the wedding there are two receptions called **Kabbalat Panim**, one for the *hatan* and one for the *kallah*. The bride and the groom are treated like a queen and king. The *kallah* is seated on a throne. The *hatan* is surrounded by guests who sing and offer toasts. Eventually the *hatan* comes to the *kallah*. Two things happen. First the *ketubah*, wedding contract, is signed. This will be given to the bride as her protection in case of divorce. The document, signed by two witnesses (not the *hatan* and *kallah)*, has the standing of a legally binding agreement. Then comes the **badeken**, the lowering of the veil by the *hatan*. The *hatan* places the veil over the *kallah's* face. This custom reminds us that Laban fooled Jacob and had Leah, not Rachel, marry Jacob. At his real marriage to Rachel, Jacob checked under the veil. The wedding takes place

under the *huppah* (canopy), which is a symbol of the home to be built and shared by the couple. It is open on all sides, just as Abraham and Sarah had their tent open all sides to welcome friends and relatives with hospitality.

Erusin (or Kiddushin)

The *hatan*, and then the *kallah*, are usually escorted to the *huppah* by their respective sets of parents. Under the *huppah*, there is a tradition that the *kallah* circles the *hatan* seven times because the world was created in seven days. Two cups of wine are used in the wedding ceremony. The first cup is used for *erusin*, the betrothal blessings, and after these are recited the couple drinks from the cup. This is also called **kiddushin**. Wine, a symbol of joy in Jewish tradition, is associated with the *Kiddush*, the sanctification prayer recited on Shabbat and festivals. Marriage, which is also called **Kiddushin**, is the sanctification of a man and woman to each other. Next the ring is given. The ring should be made of plain gold, without stones. The *hatan* now takes the wedding ring in his hand as he declares to his wife,

הֲרֵי אַתְּ מְקֻדֶּשֶׁת לִי בְּטַבַּעַת זוֹ
כְּדַת מֹשֶׁה וְיִשְׂרָאֵל.

Behold, you are made holy to me with this ring according to the laws of Moses and Israel.

Sometimes, there are two rings. The *kallah* says to the *hatan*:

הֲרֵי אַתָּה מְקֻדָּשׁ לִי בְּטַבַּעַת זוֹ
כְּדַת מֹשֶׁה וְיִשְׂרָאֵל.

Behold, you are made holy to me with this ring according to the laws of Moses and Israel.

The ring (or rings) is then placed on the forefinger of the right hand. According to Jewish law the couple is now fully married at this point. Next there is a reading of the *ketubah*. The *ketubah* is the property of the *kallah*, and she must have access to it throughout their marriage. It is often written amid beautiful artwork, to be framed and displayed in the home.

Nissuin

The reading of the *ketubah* is the break between the *Erusin/Kiddushin* (betrothal), and the **nissuin** (marriage).

The *sheva brakhot* (Seven Blessings) are now recited over the second cup of wine. These blessings link the *hatan* and *kallah* to God, the Creator of the world, the Giver of joy and love, and the ultimate Redeemer of our people. The blessings are recited by the rabbi or other people that the families wish to honor. The *hatan* and *kallah* again drink some of the wine. A glass is now placed on the floor, and the *hatan* smashes it with his foot. This is a reminder of sadness for the destruction of the Temple in Jerusalem. This marks the conclusion of the ceremony. Here is the *mazel tov*. The couple now head to the *yihud* room, their temporary private chamber.

Seudah

After the wedding is a **seudah** (a festive meal). It is a mitzvah for the guests to bring *simhah* (happiness) to the *hatan* and the *kallah* on their wedding day. There is much music and dancing as the guests celebrate with the new couple. Some guests even show off their skills at juggling and acrobatics. After the meal **Birkat Ha-Mazon** (Grace After Meals) is recited and the *Sheva Brakhot* are repeated. During the week following the wedding, it is a custom for friends and relatives to host festive meals for the bride and groom and say the *Sheva Brakhot*.

Mikvah

It is a tradition for a bride to go to the *mikvah* shortly before the wedding. Here are three texts about going to the *mikvah*. Read them and then answer the question below.

> The world's natural bodies of water—its oceans, rivers, wells, and springfed lakes—are mikvahs in their most primal form. They contain waters of divine source and thus, tradition teaches, the power to purify. Created even before the earth took shape, these bodies of water offer a prime route to consecration.
>
> *Rivkah Slonim*

> By means of immersion a person can accomplish much. Even though there is no prophecy outside of Eretz Yisrael, inside a mikvah of water there can be. Proof of this is from Ezekiel the prophet, where the Word came to him by the river Kebat, even though he was outside Eretz Yisrael...By means of the mikvah unity is created and one is able to unite his fellows' views with his own. *Beit Aharon*

> The mikvah is seen as representing a womb. Thus an individual emerging from it is as if born anew and leaves all uncleanliness behind. On another level the mikvah represents a grave. This is because when a person is submerged in water for those few moments without drawing a breath, it is as if she were in a state of non-life, and when she emerges she is like one reborn. *Mordecai Kaplan*

Why is going to *mikvah* an important preparation for a marriage?

_____

_____

_____

Building a Mikvah

The rules about building a *mikvah* are complicated. The immersion must take place in a *ma'ayan*, a spring or well. Certain rivers or lakes can therefore be used. Standard bathtubs cannot be used. Rain water can also be used and is the source of most *mikvah* water today. Though a certain amount of rainwater is required, it can be supplemented with regular tap water.

Rules for Dunking

Immersion requires that the water cover the entire body. All clothing, jewelry, and even bandages must be removed, and the hair must be combed straight so that there are no knots. In contemporary *mikvaot* for women, there is always an experienced attendant, commonly called the "mikvah lady", to watch the immersion and ensure that the woman has been entirely covered in water.

Marriage Words

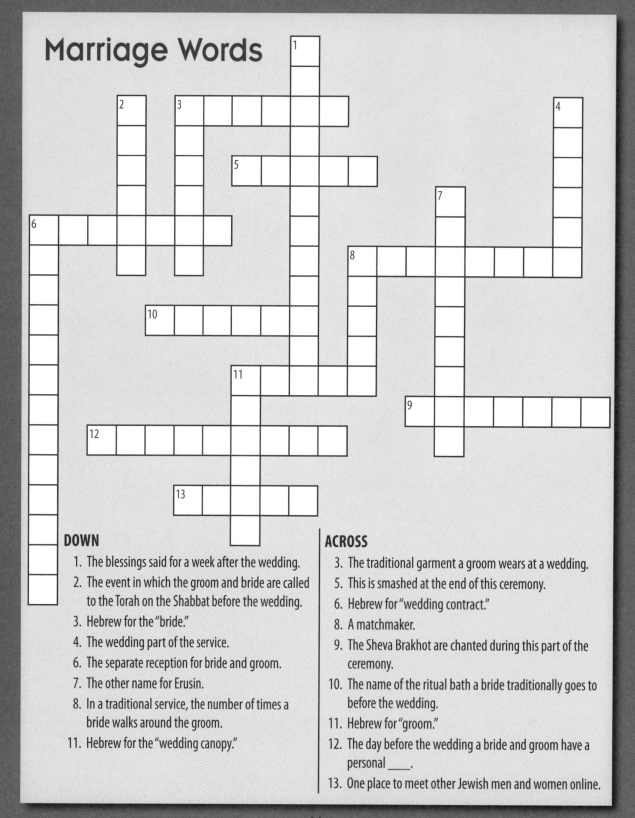

DOWN

1. The blessings said for a week after the wedding.
2. The event in which the groom and bride are called to the Torah on the Shabbat before the wedding.
3. Hebrew for the "bride."
4. The wedding part of the service.
6. The separate reception for bride and groom.
7. The other name for Erusin.
8. In a traditional service, the number of times a bride walks around the groom.
11. Hebrew for the "wedding canopy."

ACROSS

3. The traditional garment a groom wears at a wedding.
5. This is smashed at the end of this ceremony.
6. Hebrew for "wedding contract."
8. A matchmaker.
9. The Sheva Brakhot are chanted during this part of the ceremony.
10. The name of the ritual bath a bride traditionally goes to before the wedding.
11. Hebrew for "groom."
12. The day before the wedding a bride and groom have a personal ____.
13. One place to meet other Jewish men and women online.

Four Different Ketubot

Here are four different decorated *ketubot*. What are some of the common themes?

India, 1960s

Venice, Italy, 1649

Ferrara, Italy, 1775

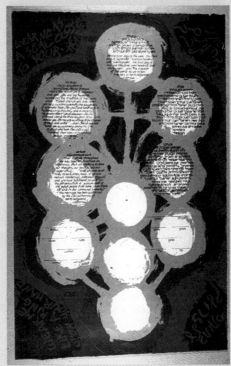

Peretz Wolf Prusan, 1978

Text of the Ketubah

Look at the text of three different kinds of *ketubot*.

Orthodox

ON THE _____ DAY OF THE WEEK, the _____ day of the month _____ in the year five thousand seven hundred and _____ since the creation of the world, the era according to which we reckon here in the city of _____ that the groom _____ son of _____ said to this bride _____ daughter of _____ .

"Be my wife according to the practice of Moses and Israel, and I will cherish, honor, support and maintain you in accordance with the custom of Jewish husbands who cherish, honor, support, and maintain their wives faithfully. And I here present you with the marriage gift of (brides), (two hundred) silver zuzim, which belong to you, according the law of Moses and Israel; and I will also give you your food, clothing and necessities, and live with you as husband and wife according to universal custom." And _____ the bride consented and became his wife... All my property, real and personal, even the shirt from my back, shall be mortgaged to secure the payment of this marriage contract in case of divorce...." _____ _____ the bridegroom, has taken upon himself the responsibility of these marriage contracts and the additions to them made for the daughters of Israel, according to the institution of our sages of blessed memory... We have followed the legal formality of symbolic delivery between _____, the son of _____, the bridegroom and _____ the daughter of _____, this bride, and we have used a garment legally fit for this purpose, to strengthen all that is stated above, and everything is valid and confirmed."

Witness _____   Witness _____

Conservative

(Texts that are the same as the Orthodox have been left out.)

…We testify that on the _____ day of the week, the _____ day of the month of _____, in the year _____, corresponding to the _____ day of _____, _____, here in _____, the groom, _____, said to the bride, _____.

"Be my wife accroding to the laws and traditions of Moses and the Jewish people. I will work on your behalf and honor, sustain, and suport you according to the practice of Jewish men, who faithfully work on behalf of their wives and honor, sustain and support them. I obligate myself to give you the sum of _____ *zuzim* as the money for your *ketubah*, to which you are entitled according to _____ law. I will provide your food, clothing and necessities, and I will live with you in marital relations according to universal custom."

The bride, _____, agreed to these terms and to become his wife, to participate together with him in establishing their home in love, harmony, peace, and companionship, according to the practice of Jewish women.

_____, the groom, and _____, the bride, furthur agreed that should either contemplate dissolution of the marriage, or following the dissolution of their marriage in the civil courts, each may summon the other to the Bet Din of the Rabbinical Assembly and the Jewish Theological Seminary, or its representative, and that each will abide by its instructions so that throughout life each will be able to live according to the laws of the Torah.

Witness _____   Witness _____

Reform

(There are many Reform *ketubah* texts. Sometimes couples write their own. The beginning that is the same as the Orthodox and Conservative, has been skipped.)

"…We pledge to be equal partners, loving friends, and supportive companions all through our life. May our love provide us with the freedom to be ourselves and the courage to follow our mutual and individual paths. As we share life's experiences, we vow to create an intimacy that will enable us to express our innermost thoughts and feelings; to be sensitive to each other's needs; to share life's joys; to comfort each other through life's sorrows; to challenge each other to achieve intellectual and physical fulfillment as well as spiritual and emotional tranquility. We will build a home together and fill it with laughter, empathy, faith, imagination, trust, friendship, companionship and love. A home in which holidays and heritage are celebrated in accordance with our Jewish culture and tradition. May we live each day as the first, the last, the only day we will have with each other. We joyfully enter into this covenant and solemnly accept the obligations herein."

Bride _____ Groom _____
Witness _____ Witness _____
Rabbi _____

Courtesy of Nishima Kaplan. www.artketubah.com

1. Who is bound by the Orthodox *ketubah*?
2. Who is bound by the Conservative *ketubah*?
3. Who is bound by a Reform *ketubah*?
4. What does each document say about divorce?
5. What does each document say about Jewish life?

Design Your Own Ketubah

Design your own *ketubah*. Write your own *ketubah* text and embellish with decorations.

Rabbi Akiva and Rachel

Rabbi Akiva was a poor and ignorant shepherd working for a rich man, Kalba Savua. Akiva was forty years old and had not studied a word of Torah. He did not even know a Hebrew letter. Rachel, Kalba Savua's daughter, fell in love with Akiva. She said to him, "If I am willing to get engaged to you, will you go to a house of study?" Akiva answered, "Yes." So they were engaged in secret. When her father learned about it he drove her out of his house and cut her off. To get even she went and married Akiva. They were so poor that they had to sleep on straw. When Rabbi Akiva picked the straw from her hair, he would say, "If I had the means, I would give you a golden hairpiece 'a Jerusalem of gold'."

The prophet Elijah came disguised as a beggar and said, "Please give me a bit of straw—my wife is about to give birth, and I have nothing for her to lie on." Rabbi

Akiva gave him some and said to his wife, "Look, this man doesn't even have the straw that we have!"

Soon Rachel told him, "Now is the time for you to go to learn Torah." He went and studied for twelve years. He had to start at the beginning. He went directly to a schoolhouse, and he and his son began reading from a child's tablet. Rabbi Akiva took hold of one end of the tablet, and his son held the other end. The teacher wrote down *alef* and *bet* for him, and he learned them; *alef* to *tav*, and he learned them; the book of Leviticus, and he learned it. He went on studying until he learned the whole Torah. At the end of twelve years he had become a leading scholar. He returned home, bringing with him twelve thousand disciples. The whole town went out to meet him. Rachel went out to meet him, too. When she came near him, she fell upon her face and was about to kiss his feet. The disciples started to push her out of the way. Rabbi Akiva shouted at them, "Let her be—all I have and all that you have really belongs to her."

Her father fell upon his face before Rabbi Akiva. He gave Rabbi Akiva half of his wealth. Rabbi Akiva bought Rachel, his wife, a "Jerusalem of Gold" (Avot de Rabbi Natan 6, 12).

1. What does this story teach us about the connection between love and Torah?
2. How does Rachel's love help Rabbi Akiva become a scholar?
3. What does this story teach about marriage?

The Marriage Service

The *ketubah* is read and signed and the <u>h</u>atan lowers the veil of the *kallah*. It is a tradition to perform a ceremony called **kinyan** before the *ketubah* is signed. *Kinyan* is when the <u>h</u>atan pulls on a handkerchief held by the *kallah*'s father.

Erusin

When the <u>h</u>atan reaches the <u>h</u>uppah the <u>h</u>azan sings:

<u>H</u>azan: Blessed be the One who comes in the name of the Eternal: we bless you out of the house of the Eternal. (Psalms 188.26)

O come, let us worship and bow down; let us kneel before the Eternal, our Maker. (Psalms 95.6)

Serve the Eternal with joy. Come before God with praising. (Psalms 100.2)

The One who is mighty, blessed and great above all beings, may God bless the bridegroom and the bride.

When the *kallah* nears the <u>h</u>uppah, the <u>h</u>atan walks to meet her. She then circles the <u>h</u>atan as the <u>h</u>azan sings:

<u>H</u>azan: Blessed is she who has come. The One who understands the speech of the rose among thorns, the love of a *kallah* who is the joy of her beloved— May God bless <u>h</u>atan and *kallah*.

The rabbi may first offer a brief prayer or teaching. Then the rabbi holds a cup of wine and recites:

Rabbi: Blessed are You, Eternal, our God, Ruler of the Cosmos, the One Who creates the fruit of the vine.

Congregation: Amen

Rabbi: As you share this cup of wine, so may you share all things from this day on with love and with understanding.

Blessed are You, Eternal, our God, Ruler of the Cosmos, Who has made us holy with Your *mitzvot*, and has permitted us to wed under the <u>h</u>uppah and enter the sacred covenant of marriage. Blessed are You, Eternal, Who has made your people Israel holy by the ritual of the <u>h</u>uppah and the sacred covenant of marriage.

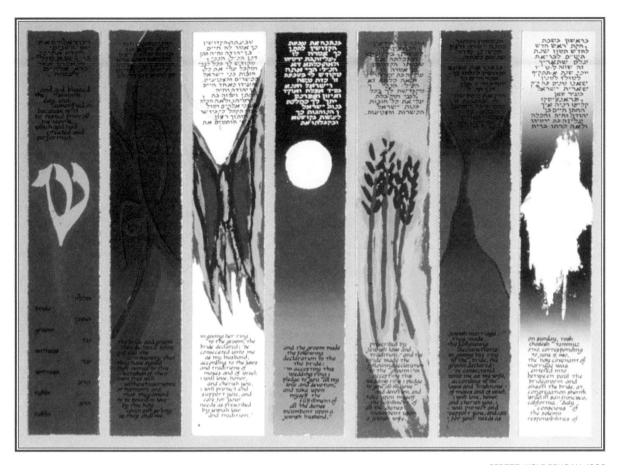

PERETZ WOLF PRUSAN, 1980

Hatan and *kallah* both drink from the cup of wine. The *hatan* places the ring upon the forefinger of the right hand of the *kallah,* and says:

Hatan: הֲרֵי אַתְּ מְקֻדֶּשֶׁת לִי בְּטַבַּעַת זוֹ כְּדַת מֹשֶׁה וְיִשְׂרָאֵל

> Behold, you are made holy to me with this ring according to the laws of Moses and Israel.

The *kallah* places the ring upon the forefinger of the right hand of the *hatan* and says:

Kallah: הֲרֵי אַתָּה מְקֻדָּשׁ לִי בְּטַבַּעַת זוֹ כְּדַת מֹשֶׁה וְיִשְׂרָאֵל

> Behold, you are made holy to me with this ring according to the laws of Moses and Israel.

73

Nissuin

The *ketubah* is read. A second cup of wine is poured and the *Sheva Brakhot* (7 blessings) are said.

Rabbi /Hazan: [1] Blessed are You, Eternal our God, Ruler of the Cosmos, Who created the fruit of the vine.

[2] Blessed are You, Eternal our God, Ruler of the Cosmos, Who has created all things for Your own glory.

[3] Blessed are You, Eternal our God, Ruler of the Cosmos, Creator of people.

[4] Blessed are You, Eternal our God, Ruler of the cosmos, Who has made people in Your image, after Your likeness, and has prepared for them, out of the Divine self, a piece of eternity. Blessed are You, Eternal, Creator of people.

[5] May Jerusalem be exceedingly glad and celebrate, when her children are gathered within her in joy. Blessed are You, Eternal, Who makes Jerusalem joyful through her children.

[6] O make this loving couple to gladly rejoice, even as of old You did gladden Your creations in the garden of Eden. Blessed are You, Eternal, Who makes *hatan* and *kallah* rejoice.

[7] Blessed are You, Eternal our God, Ruler of the Cosmos, Who has created joy and gladness, *hatan* and kallah, happiness and celebration, pleasure and delight, love, human connection, peace and fellowship. Soon may there be heard in the cities of Judah, and in the streets of Jerusalem, the voice of joy and gladness, the voice of the *hatan* and the voice of the *kallah*, the happy voice of *hatanim* from their *huppot*, and of youths from their feasts of song. Blessed are You, Eternal, Who makes *hatan* to rejoice with the *kallah*.

The *hatan* and *kallah* drink from the second glass of wine. A glass is broken by the *hatan*.

Congregation: *Mazel tov.*

The *hatan* and *kallah* head for some private time and then join everyone else at the wedding feast where the *Sheva Brakhot* are said again.

X-Raying the Sheva Brakhot

The *Sheva Brakhot* are divided into three parts. The structure helps us to see this. A long blessing is one that both begins and ends with a sentence that begins "Praised are You…" Find the two long *brakhot* in the *Sheva Brakhot*.

1. The first *brakhah*, the blessing over wine, is a _____ .

2. The next three *brakhot* (2, 3, and 4) are connected. They all share the theme of _____

   _____ .

3. The last three *brakhot* (5, 6, and 7) are connected. They all share the theme of _____

   _____ .

4. Some of the *brakhot* include references to Adam and Eve. What is the connection

   between Adam and Eve and a wedding? _____

5. The fifth and seventh *brakhot* add in the image of Jerusalem. Jerusalem also comes into

   the wedding with the breaking of the glass at the end. What is the connection between

   Jerusalem and a wedding?_____

   _____

6. What lessons about marriage do you think the *Sheva Brakhot* teach?_____

   _____

Commitment Ceremonies

Perhaps the hottest argument in the United States is about "same-sex marriage." Some people look at the Bible (and the Talmud) and say that God forbids same-sex relationships. Others read those same sources and believe that God thinks that all loving relationships are holy. This issue has become part of presidential debates and part of elections in many states. It is also hotly debated among Jews.

Some Jews, some rabbis, and some synagogues believe that the Bible (and the Talmud) limits marriage to couples made up of men and women. Other Jews, other rabbis and other synagogues accept same-sex couples and offer them the chance to make their relationships permanent. Commitment ceremonies are the way that gay and lesbian couples make their relationships permanent.

This debate will not be quickly resolved. Both sides believe that this issue is a matter of ethics. The problem is that both sides apply different values to solve this same ethical problem. As a class, discuss some of the values that are involved. Find out the position of your rabbi(s) and congregation.

© CATHERINE KARNOW/CORBIS

76

Growing Old

© TURBO/ZEFA/CORBIS

Until 120

According to the midrash, Moses lived 120 years, the perfect length for a life. We are told that he lived forty years in Egypt until he killed the slave master and had to run away; forty years in Midian as a shepherd; and forty years leading the Jewish people out of Egypt and in the wilderness.

How would you describe each of the periods of his life?

1–40: _____

40–80: _____

80–120: _____

Why did Moses need eighty years of preparation before he was ready to lead?
Why did Israel need an elder to be its leader?

Respecting the Elderly

In the Torah you will find this verse:

> *Before the gray-haired you shall stand up and you shall give honor to the presence of the elderly and you shall revere your God. I am the Eternal* (Leviticus 19.32).

Because of this verse it is a mitzvah to stand whenever an elderly person enters a room. It is also a mitzvah to rise when a scholar enters a room. Sefer Ḥinukh expains that an eldery person is one who has collected wisdom.

Besides standing, list five ways of respecting the elderly.

1. _____
   _____

2. _____
   _____

3. _____
   _____

4. _____
   _____

5. _____
   _____

© KAZUYOSHI NOMACHI/CORBIS

The Meaning of Old

© SHOOT/ZEFA/CORBIS

On August 14, 1935, the Social Security Act was signed into a law. It gave retirement benefits to anyone reaching the age of sixty-five. It was a good plan, because in 1935 almost no one reached sixty-five. Then, sixty-five was really old. Today seventy-year-olds regularly play golf or go to Pilates class. Old is much older than it once was. It is now not unusual for people to live into their late eighties or even nineties.

This longer life span makes a big difference in Jewish life. There are programs like **Elderhostel,** in which seniors go to a university and study for a week. Adult education classes and weekly Torah studies are filled with empty nesters (people whose children have grown up and left home). Many daily *minyanim* are also maintained by people we would consider to be "senior citizens."

With more Jews living longer, there are also some problems. More and more Jews are living on fixed incomes and more can be considered poor. As people get to be very old they often need assisted living or even nursing homes, and the Jewish community is building more and more residences to meet this need.

Pirke Avot 5.24

Five is the age for the study of Torah; ten is the age-for the study of Mishnah; thirteen is the age for becoming subject to the mitzvot; fifteen is the age for the study of Talmud; eighteen is the age for the bridal canopy; twenty is the age for pursuing a living; thirty is the age for full strength; forty is the age for understanding; fifty is the age for being able to give counsel; sixty is the age for being mature, seventy is the age for respect, eighty is the age of strength; ninety is the age for a bent body; at the age of one hundred, one is as good as dead.

What does this text say about what children should do?

What does it say that adults should do?

What does it say about growing old?

Death

This is the text of a prayer called *Eil Malei Rahamin*. It is the heart of both a funeral and a of a *Yizkor,* memorial service. Read its text

God of compassion,
grant perfect peace in Your sheltering Presence,
among the holy and the pure who shine in the brightness of the firmament,
to the soul of our dear _____ who has gone to his/her eternal rest.

God of compassion,
remember all his/her worthy deeds in the land of the living.
May his/her soul be bound up in the bond of everlasting life.
May God be his/her inheritance.
May s/he rest in peace.
And let us answer: Amen.

1. What does this prayer say about God?
2. What does it say about death?
3. What does it say about life?

The Jewish Way of Death

A Jewish Death

Death scares and saddens almost everyone. It also interests us because death comes with a lot of unanswerable questions. Judaism comes with lots of rituals that make the death of a friend or relative easier to tolerate. It also has a number of understandings that may give you workable answers to many of the questions.

If one is conscious and aware that one is dying, one says a *vidui*, a mini-confessional that is like a very short Yom Kippur. Then one says the Shema, which are supposed to be a Jew's last words.

Preparations for a Funeral

Traditionally, a dead body was taken care of by a **Hevra Kaddisha**, a burial society. They are members of the community who volunteer to do *mitzvat met*, the mitzvah of taking care of the dead. They wash and dress the dead. They wrap the body in the *kittel*, the white robe acquired at marriage. They care for the dead and make sure there is a **shomer**, a guardian. A dead body is never left alone before the burial. Today, many Jews use a professional undertaker to do these jobs.

The Jewish tradition encourages mourners to have the burial take place as soon after the death as possible.

© FATIH SARIBAS/REUTERS/CORBIS

Traditionally a Jew is buried in a wooden box with no nails. Nothing is done to preserve the body. The Torah says that a person goes from dust to dust, and traditionally we do nothing to keep a body from returning to dust.

Between the death and the funeral, the mourners are considered to be *onanim*. *Onanim* have no responsibilities Jewishly. This means that *onanim* are excused from things like daily services that are considered to be *mitzvot*.

The Funeral and Burial

Before the funeral there is a ceremony called *k'riah*, the tearing. Originally a family member or close friend would rip his or her garment upon learning

that a person had died. At the same time, he or she would say, "*Barukh Dayan ha-Emet*," which essentially means "God is fair." Today the ripping has been replaced by the cutting of a black ribbon that is pinned on.

A Jewish funeral usually happens in two parts. First there is the funeral; then there is the burial. One usually happens in a synagogue or chapel, the second happens at the graveside.

There is no specific structure for a funeral. Often a Psalm or some prayer is recited. Very often the Twenty-third Psalm ("The Eternal is my shepherd…") is used. Then there is a *hesped*. In English this is called a eulogy. It is a speech about the person who has died that recalls the good things he or she has done. It is designed to bring comfort to the mourners. The service ends with *El malei rahamin*. Another prayer called *tzeduk ha-Din* (Righteous Judgment) is usually part of the service. At the very end, the *Kaddish* is said.

Once the casket is lowered in the ground, a shovel is made avaliable. Each person at the funeral uses the back side of the shovel to throw a little dirt into the grave. When leaving, those at the funeral shake the hand of, or hug, the mourners. It is tradition to say: *Ha-Makon yenakhem etkhem, b'Tokh sh'Ar avelei Zion v'Yerushalayim*, which means "May God comfort you, along with the other mourners of Zion and Jerusalem."

After the funeral they enter the status of *aveilut* (official mourning) and the mourners go home. In olden times, their neighbors would make sure that a meal was waiting for them. Today, for the most part, friends or a synagogue committee make sure that there is food in the house for a first meal and food for the rest of the week. This first meal is called a *seudat havra'ah*. It usually contains an egg, a symbol of life. Now the formal mourning begins.

The Periods of Mourning

The first seven days are called *Shiva*. *Shiva* means seven. Traditionally, mourners would stay home for seven days following the funeral and let the community take care of them. Food was brought in. The *minyan* (the ten people needed to hold a service where *kaddish* is said) was brought to them. Today, many Jews sit *shiva* for less than seven days.

Sh'loshim (thirty days) is the next mourning period. Like *shiva,* it starts on the day of the funeral. It goes for thirty days. After *shiva* is over, people go back to work, back to their normal lives. But during *sh'loshim*, they do not go to parties or celebrations.

Shanah means "year." *Shanah* is the next period of morning. *Shanah* lasts for eleven months following the funeral. During this time mourners continue to say *kaddish*. After *shanah* is completed, *kaddish* is only said at *yahrzeit*, the anniversary of the death. Some time after *shana* is completed, the family visits the cemetery and **unveils** the headstone that marks the grave. *Kaddish* is a prayer that is said, according to midrash, as a way of getting our beloved relatives eternal life. *Shanah* lasts less than a calendar year because none of our relatives could be so bad as to need a whole year of praying.

Mourning Stages

The stages of mourning help to move a person from deep sorrow and anger back towards leading a normal life. Fill in this chart.

	Before funeral	Shiva	Sheloshim	Shanah	After Shanah	Yahrzeit
No responsibilities						
Food brought to mourners						
Mourners stay at home						
Kaddish is said						
Daily minyan at home						
No parties						
A time to mourn						

What does each stage do to help a person move from a mourner back to a normal life.

Before the funeral: _____

Shiva: _____

Sheloshim: _____

Shanah: _____

After Shanah: _____

Yahrzeit: _____

Why We Say Kaddish for Only Eleven Months

This story is the origin of the use of *kaddish* as a mourning prayer. It started out as something said at the end of study sessions.

Rabbi Akiva was walking through a cemetery. He saw a naked man, covered in soot, carrying a huge bundle of wood on his head. The man was running. He was shouting "I'm late. I'm late. If I don't finish they will make it worse." Rabbi Akiva asked the man, "Is there anything I can do to help? If you are poor, can I buy you out of this debt to these masters who are way too demanding?" The man said, "You are talking to a dead man. I am in *Gehinom*, the place one waits before going on to the Garden of Eden. I will be here forever. Every night they boil me in oil using the wood I collect."

Rabbi Akiva asked, "What is your name?" The man answered, "Akiva." The rabbi asked further, "What was your crime? What will help you to move on?" The man answered, "I was a tax collector, and I took bribes from the rich and overtaxed the poor. They told me that my only way out of *Gehinom* was for a child of mine to say the *kaddish*. I need that child to count as one of my good deeds." In those days one said the *kaddish* only at the end of Torah study. It was not a mourner's prayer. The person with the best Torah insight led it.

Rabbi Akiva left Akiva and went looking for a child. He found a son. The son was living as a non-Jew. He did not know even one Hebrew letter. The Jewish community had abandoned him. Rabbi Akiva began to teach him, but the son's heart was not in his studies. Rabbi Akiva tried all his best teacher tricks—nothing worked.

Rabbi Akiva prayed to God and asked for the child's heart to be opened. Slowly the lessons went better. Once, when Rabbi Akiva brought the son to a Torah study, the son was picked to lead the *kaddish*. When the prayer was over, Akiva went to the Garden of Eden.

That night Rabbi Akiva had a dream. In the dream he heard Akiva's voice. "You saved me from Gehinom. May your soul go quickly to the Garden of Eden in its time." In his dream, Rabbi Akiva said, "Eternal, Your NAME lasts forever, Your memory is for all generations" (Ps 102.13). This is when the mourner's *kaddish* began.

(Mahzor Vitry)

1. According to this story, what does the *kaddish* do for the dead person?
2. According to this story, what does the *kaddish* do for the person who says it?
3. Why do you think we say *kaddish* for only eleven months?

What Happens After We Die?

Jews have lots of different beliefs about what happens after you die. Here are some of them.

Gehinom* then Gan Eden:** The story we read about the *kaddish* was the most popular belief in the past. That after you died you went to a place called *Gehinom* where God worked out a program to help you repent the stuff you couldn't do when you were alive. Then when you were the best possible you, you went to ***Gan Eden (the Garden of Eden). This is the Jewish version of heaven and hell. Really bad people never left *Gehinom*.

Resurrection of the Dead: The most popular Jewish belief in the past was that God would put your body back together, reinsert your soul, and you would live again.

Soul Goes Back to God: One of the most popular Jewish beliefs today is that after you die your soul becomes part of God again.

Dead is Dead: Another popular modern belief is that nothing happens to you after you die, but your memory lives on in the memory of the good things you did. Life after death happens when you influence and affect other people.

Reincarnation: A lot of people don't know it, but there is a Jewish belief in reincarnation. Reincarnation is when, after you die, your soul is reborn as another person. In the Kabbalah this is known as *Gilui Nefashot*.

The Kaddish

Let God's Great NAME be (1) BIG and (2) HOLY	יִתְגַּדַּל וְיִתְקַדַּשׁ שְׁמֵהּ רַבָּא	1.
in this world that God CREATED with will.	בְּעָלְמָא דִּי בְרָא כִרְעוּתֵהּ	2.
Let God completely RULE the EMPIRE	וְיַמְלִיךְ מַלְכוּתֵהּ	3.
in this life and in these days,	בְּחַיֵּיכוֹן וּבְיוֹמֵיכוֹן	4.
and in the lifetime of all the Families-of-Israel.	וּבְחַיֵּי דְכָל־בֵּית יִשְׂרָאֵל	5.
Let this happen QUICKLY in a nearby time	בַּעֲגָלָא וּבִזְמַן קָרִיב	6.
and let us say: "AMEN."	וְאִמְרוּ אָמֵן.	7.
Let God's Great NAME be blessed	יְהֵא שְׁמֵהּ רַבָּא מְבָרַךְ	8.
in the world and in the world of worlds—FOREVER.	לְעָלַם וּלְעָלְמֵי עָלְמַיָּא.	9.
(3) Blessed, (4) Called AMAZING, (5) Glorified	יִתְבָּרַךְ וְיִשְׁתַּבַּח וְיִתְפָּאַר	10.
(6) Extolled, (7) Honored, (8) Respected,	וְיִתְרוֹמַם וְיִתְנַשֵּׂא וְיִתְהַדָּר	11.
(9) Lifted Up and (10) HALLELUYAHed	וְיִתְעַלֶּה וְיִתְהַלָּל	12.
be the NAME of the Holy-ONE-Who-is-to-be-Blessed	שְׁמֵהּ דְּקֻדְשָׁא בְּרִיךְ הוּא	13.
above anything we can Bless and Sing	לְעֵלָּא מִן כָּל־בִּרְכָתָא וְשִׁירָתָא	14.
above all prayers and consolations	תֻּשְׁבְּחָתָא וְנֶחֱמָתָא	15.
that we can say in this world. And let us say, "AMEN."	דַּאֲמִירָן בְּעָלְמָא וְאִמְרוּ אָמֵן.	16.
Let there be a great PEACE from heaven.	יְהֵא שְׁלָמָא רַבָּא מִן שְׁמַיָּא	17.
Let us have a good life—and the same for all of Israel	וְחַיִּים עָלֵינוּ וְעַל כָּל־יִשְׂרָאֵל	18.
and let us say: "Amen."	וְאִמְרוּ אָמֵן.	19.
May the One-Who-Makes PEACE in the heavens above	עוֹשֶׂה שָׁלוֹם בִּמְרוֹמָיו	20.
May that One make PEACE for us	הוּא יַעֲשֶׂה שָׁלוֹם עָלֵינוּ	21.
and for all of Israel and let us say: "AMEN."	וְעַל כָּל־יִשְׂרָאֵל וְאִמְרוּ אָמֵן.	22.

1. What is the theme of this prayer?
2. Why is it used for mourners?

Ethical Wills

There is a Jewish tradition for parents to write ethical wills (as well as financial wills) for their children. An ethical will is a statement of the way a parent wants his or her children to live. Here is an example.

The Testament of Eleazar of Mayence

Germany, about 1357

These are the things which my sons and daughters shall do at my request. They shall go to the house of prayer morning and evening, and shall pay special regard to the *Amidah* and the *Shema*. As soon as the service is over, they shall occupy themselves a little with the Torah, the Psalms, or with works of charity. Their business must be conducted honestly, in their dealings both with Jew and Gentile. They must be gentle in their manners and quick to respond to every honorable request. They must not talk more than is necessary; by this will they be saved from slander, lying, and silliness. They shall…never turn away a poor man empty-handed, but must give him what they can, be it much or little. If one begs a lodging overnight, and you know him or her not, provide the funds to pay an innkeeper. Satisfy the needs of the poor in every possible way....

If they can by any means contrive it, my sons and daughters should live in communities, and not isolated from other Jews, so that their sons and daughters may learn the ways of Judaism. Even if compelled to solicit from others the money to pay a teacher, they must not let the young of both sexes go without instruction in the Torah…

I earnestly beg my children to be tolerant and humble to all…Should cause for dissension present itself, be slow to accept the quarrel; seek peace and pursue it with all the strength you posses…

On holidays and festivals and Sabbaths seek to make happy the poor, the unfortunate, widows and orphans, who should always be guests at your tables; their joyous entertainment is a *mitzvah*. Let me repeat my warning against gossip and scandal. And as you speak no gossip, listen to none; for if there were no receivers there would be no bearers of slanderous tales…. (Jacob Marcus, *The Jew in the Medieval World: A Sourcebook, 315-1791*

List some of the big ideas that this father was trying to share with his children. _____
_____
_____

Your Ethical Will

Explain to your parents the idea of an ethical will. Have them list ten things they would like you to have as part of the way you live.

1. _____

2. _____

3. _____

4. _____

5. _____

Memorial Papercut, 1903

© LANE YERKES

Dream Kaddish

An old woman is in her bedroom in Prague. The angel of death enters and gets ready to take her. She says, "Not yet." He says, "What's wrong?" She says, "I was the maid for the rabbi, and the community takes good care of me, but I need someone to say קַדִּישׁ for me." The angel asked, "Do you have a relative?" The woman answered, "I have a great-grandson whom I have never met. He lives in Germany." "That can be arranged," said the angel.

That night the woman died. The people of Prague found her with a big smile on her face. That night Joseph, her great-grandson, had a dream. In that dream an old woman in white appeared. She put his face in her hands and said, "I am your great-grandmother. Say *kaddish* for me. There is no one else to do it but you."

Joseph woke in the morning. He barely remembered the old woman who lived in Prague. He had nothing to do with his family anymore. He had nothing to do with the Jewish people either. He went to his dresser and took out his *bar mitzvah tallit*. He had not thought about it in years. He took it and started to walk.

He walked and walked through the city, through the forest, past fields, not knowing where he was going, but knowing where he should go. He came to a small Jewish village and made his way to the synagogue. He told his story to the *shamash*, the spiritual custodian of the *shul*. The *shamash* taught him the words of the *kaddish*. He said it every day for eleven months.

When the year was over many things had changed. Joseph had sold his apartment in the city and moved to this village. He became part of the community. He met a woman, and they were ready to get married. In saying *kaddish* Joseph found his way back to his people.

(Based on "Amen" in *Ze Zidovskeho Ghetta* by A. Hoffman and R. Heuerova, found in *Jewish Tales from Eastern Europe*, Nadia Grosser Nagarajan)

1. What did the *kaddish* do for the great grandmother? What did it do for Joseph?

2. What does this story teach about saying the mourner's *kaddish*?

3. How can remembering this story help you know where to point your heart when you participate in the mourner's *kaddish*?

How to Visit a Shiva House

It is a mitzvah to comfort mourners. We perform this mitzvah by attending the funeral and we perform it by visiting the *shiva* house.

While it is sometimes hard or scary to try to find the right words to say to a person who has faced a death in his or her life, the Jewish tradition makes it easy to know what to do.

Here are some of the traditions you will find at a *shiva* house. You many not find all of them at every *shiva* house.

- No one comes to a *shiva* house without bringing some food. This lets you head to the kitchen and talk to other people there.

- Usually the door to the house of mourning is left open so that no one needs to ring a bell or knock. This also means that the mourners do not have to act as hosts, opening the door and welcoming people.

- Sometimes you will find a row of shoes outside the door. This means you take yours off, too.

- You need not say anything to the mourners. Just being there is enough. If you have to do something, a handshake or a hug is great.

- Follow the mood. If people are sitting quietly, sit quietly. If people are telling stories and memories about the person who died, perhaps you can tell one. This is not a time to entertain. It is just a time to be there.

- There may be a service when you are there. Your job is to join in and respond to the *kaddish* as it is said by the mourners.

- When you are ready to leave, you can just leave. There is no need to say goodbye. The mourners need not come to the door and see you off. They need not interrupt their conversations to say goodbye or thank you. You have done your *mitzvah*. Now, just leave.

What is the wisdom in these customs? Whom do they help? The mourners? The visitors? How does this work?

Why I Joined Our <u>H</u>evra Kaddisha

How one woman, in the middle of her own year of mourning, joined this "holy society" of those who prepare the dead for burial— and what it has meant to her.

By Judy Freudenstein

I remember from my childhood days in a small German Jewish community that the <u>Hevra</u> *Kadisha*—literally, "holy fellowship"; in fact, the Jewish burial society—was looked upon with great respect and admiration. Even as children we were conscious of the sense of dedication that was needed to overcome inconvenience and squeamishness to carry out the tasks of the <u>Hevra</u> at short notice and at any hour. It was considered a great honor to be asked to join this group. Their work was strictly *l'shem mitzvah* [for the sake of the mitzvah—commandment—itself], that is to say, without any compensation.

I was asked to join the Riverdale *Hevra Kadisha* the year that my father died. I had mixed feelings about joining, probably because of our fresh personal loss and the three years of sickness that preceded it.

I Didn't Want to Become Hardened to the Dead

Up until then, in the absence of a Ladies' *Hevra* of *shul* members, our congregation had been forced to call upon a group of women from Williamsburg who do this kind of work regularly for a livelihood. These were committed women, but they were hardened by the daily exposure. We all felt that the first law of the *Hevra* is to treat the dead with the same tenderness as though they were alive.

Each Taharah is Suffering, but the First Was a Lesson

My first *taharah* ["purification," or preparing the body] was a young woman. I remember clearly thinking that this was unfair. My first experience with this *mitzvah* should have been

an aged person who had lived out a full life, where death would come at a more easily acceptable time. But at the same time I realized that this was not realistic thinking, because in this game one cannot choose. Again I felt that if I would decline on the grounds that it was to be my first encounter with a corpse and that I was not ready to meet with a young woman, snatched away in her prime and deformed by years of illness, I would rob myself of an experience that would touch me and maybe in some way add some dimension to my life now or later.

Since this first tragic *taharah*, I have been called whenever the *Hevra* was needed. Each time, before the actual *taharah*, the body is lifted off the bed onto a wooden board ("*Abheben*"). The *taharah*—nowadays usually performed in a specially equipped room in the funeral parlor—consists essentially of carefully cleaning the body, including trimming nails and combing hair. This is followed by a ceremonial purification with nine measures of water. Finally the body is carefully dried, clothed in white linen garments and placed in the casket. A bag with earth from the land of Israel is placed under the head. The details are governed by *halakhah* [Jewish law] and by customs which may vary slightly in different communities.

Reprinted with permission from the author